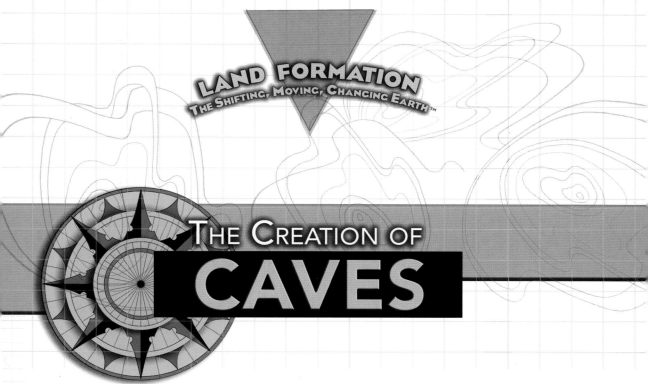

LAND FORMATION
THE SHIFTING, MOVING, CHANGING EARTH™

THE CREATION OF
CAVES

J. Elizabeth Mills

rosen publishing's
rosen
central®

New York

To cavers and adventurers everywhere—your curiosity and courage inspire me

Published in 2010 by The Rosen Publishing Group, Inc.
29 East 21st Street, New York, NY 10010

First Edition

Library of Congress Cataloging-in-Publication Data

Mills, J. Elizabeth.
The creation of caves / J. Elizabeth Mills.
    p. cm. (Land formation: the shifting, moving, changing earth)
Includes bibliographical references and index.
ISBN-13: 978-1-4358-5297-6 (library binding)
ISBN-13: 978-1-4358-5592-2 (pbk)
ISBN-13: 978-1-4358-5593-9 (6-pack)
1. Caves—Juvenile literature. I. Title.
GB601.2.M55 2010
551.44'7—dc22

2008051937

Manufactured in Malaysia

On the cover: Ha Long Bay, in Vietnam, is filled with thousands of limestone caves. Its name means "Descending Dragon Bay."

CONTENTS

INTRODUCTION

Caves are perhaps the last areas on earth that have not been fully explored yet. They are buried deep beneath the earth, inside mountains, within frozen glaciers, and under the sea. They nurture a hidden wilderness of life that could survive nowhere else. Amazing rock formations hang, twist, bubble, bloom, and float in a breathtaking display of frozen artistry. Animals rest and roost within the shelter of cave walls and swarm out to find food, sustaining a delicate food chain.

Each cave's vaulted chambers, labyrinthine passageways, and bizarre creatures hold clues both to our ancestry and to our future as a planet. Who were the first people to live in a cave? Who are the people who still live in caves? These are questions speleologists—scientists who study caves—strive to answer through their expeditions.

The cleanliness of our water and air and the change in our climate all affect caves and the animals that live within them. We have a responsibility to protect this planet for future generations to explore and appreciate. Heed the caver's motto: "Take nothing but pictures, leave nothing but footprints, kill nothing but time."

Carlsbad Caverns, in New Mexico, is full of rooms like this one, called the Chinese Theater, with all kinds of unusual rock formations.

WHAT IS A CAVE?

A cave is a natural opening in the earth that leads to underground chambers. Caves can be many different sizes and shapes. A large cave is called a cavern, and a narrow opening is called a crevice. There are four main kinds of caves: solution, glacier, lava, and sea caves. No two caves are exactly alike. Some are shallow and easy to explore. Others twist and wind through long, dark, endless passageways.

Water is responsible for forming most of the caves we know, in one way or another. Underground rivers seep into rocky cracks and eat away at the stone. Cold water from melted glaciers burrows through the ice to make frozen tunnels, and ocean waves pound and carve out rocky shores. Sometimes, as in the case of solution caves, the water contains minerals and acids that help it sculpt and shape the rock.

Let's take a look at how caves are made and how each kind is unique.

Solution Caves

The most common type of cave is called a solution cave. This kind of cave can form from either limestone or sandstone.

Limestone covers about 10 percent of the earth's surface. It is a sedimentary rock that contains the shells and skeletons of tiny marine animals that lived millions of years ago.

Once, this rock was at the bottom of shallow seas, which were filled with marine animals. When the animals died, their shells and bodies floated to the sea floor and were crushed as more and more shells and bodies piled on top of them. This pressure, and various chemicals in the water, compacted the layers into reefs that are similar to modern coral reefs but thicker and larger.

As millions of years pass, earthquakes and volcanoes reshape the landscape and lower the sea level, exposing the limestone. Forests grow on top of the rocks, creating cracks in the surface that allow rainwater to enter. As the water passes through soil on its way into the rock, it picks up carbon dioxide, a gas present in the atmosphere. This gas turns the water into carbonic acid, enabling it to erode—or eat away at—the limestone more easily.

Carving a Maze

Over the course of thousands of years, the force of the moving water dissolves more and more limestone. Crevices become tunnels, which in turn become caves, and then huge caverns. As the cracks get bigger, more water can flow, turning these small streams into underground rivers.

When a stream flows straight downward along a crack, it creates a vertical shaft. Some vertical shafts are immense, plummeting down hundreds of feet into complete darkness.

When a stream flows at an angle, it creates a maze of twisting tunnels that meet in a flooded area called a water table. A water

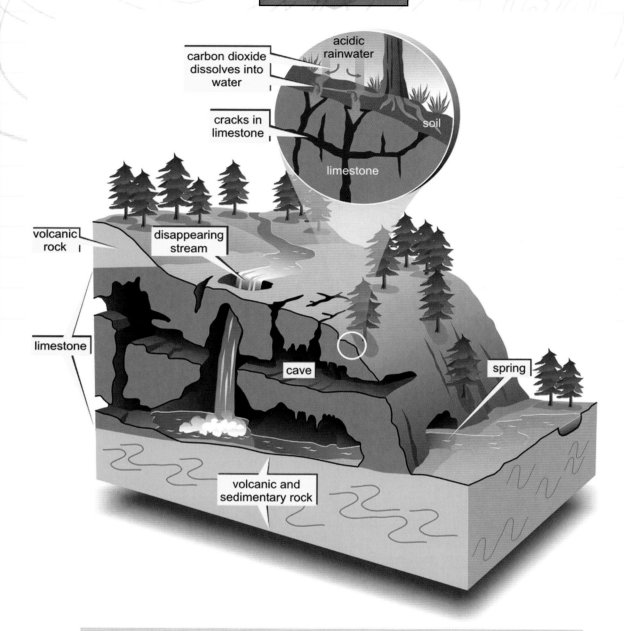

carbon dioxide dissolves into water

acidic rainwater

cracks in limestone

soil

limestone

volcanic rock

disappearing stream

limestone

cave

spring

volcanic and sedimentary rock

In this diagram, you can follow a stream as it cuts its way into limestone and carves out underground caves.

table occurs when the rock is saturated, or completely full, of water. Just below the water table, streams of carbonic acid continue to erode passages until they reach springs in nearby valleys.

In the cave, tunnels join other tunnels and form enormous chambers. The larger the chambers are, the more water they can hold, and more water means more erosion. But at a certain point, the level of the water table lowers, and the cave cannot get any bigger. As the water empties out, cave formations begin to grow. We'll take a look at them in the next chapter.

Caves that are created in passages filled with water are called phreatic caves. As water continues to move through and enlarge the cave, the floor level drops, and there is a layer of air above the water. This kind of cave is called a vadose cave. Some vadose caves are even completely dry. As a cave continues to enlarge, sometimes the roof will collapse, opening up a larger chamber.

Sulfur Caves

Some solution caves are created not by rainwater but by water from within the earth. This water contains hydrogen sulfide, a gas that smells like rotten eggs. This gas is present in areas that have oil or gas underground. Bacteria called extremophiles, which earn their name by growing in extreme conditions, feed on the oil and gas and produce hydrogen sulfide. The gas seeps up into the rock and mixes with the oxygen in water to make sulfuric acid. This acid is much more powerful than carbonic acid and dissolves the rock quickly and dramatically, leaving behind strange cave formations and unexpected passageways.

In many cases, the easiest and best way to find a sand-stone cave is by kayak.

Sandstone Caves

Sandstone caves are less common than limestone caves. These form when water carves into soft sandstone rocks.

Sandstone is also a sedimentary rock. While limestone forms from skeletons of ancient marine animals, sandstone forms when layers of sand are cemented together under great heat and pressure for millions of years.

This type of rock is commonly found in the southwestern part of the United States. Long ago, rivers formed deep canyons

KARST LANDSCAPES

Karst is a region of soluble bedrock, such as limestone or dolomite, that has been dissolved and eroded by underground streams. These streams enter through openings like potholes and sinkholes, and they carve out passageways and caverns in the limestone. Karst makes up 20 percent of the land in the United States, and karst aquifers provide 25 percent of the nation's drinking water. However, these sources of water are fragile. Many caves and sinkholes have been contaminated by trash, pesticides, human waste, and other polluting agents. We must understand the significance of these regions so that we can protect them and keep our water clean!

between high cliffs. At the base of these cliffs, the constant flowing water dug out shallow caves. The rivers continued to slice into the canyons, making the caves even deeper and pushing them up the hills. As the caves became exposed to wind, strong gales blew about the sandstone particles, further grinding the caves into the hillsides. Some Native Americans used these caves as temporary or even permanent shelters, and many artifacts have been found inside.

Lava Caves

The hottest caves are located near volcanoes. But these caves aren't formed by dissolved rock and water. Instead, they are formed by the lava itself. When a volcano erupts, hot molten lava

shoots out of the opening and spews down the sides of the volcano in channels. These channels look like long red fingers. As lava moves away from the volcano's heat, the surface of the lava moves more slowly than the interior of the lava flow, which continues to move rapidly. The sides of the lava river cool first, and then the

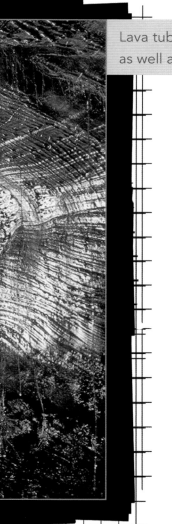

Lava tubes are filled with cooled lava strings and bubbly floors, as well as their own stalagmites and stalactites.

surface cools, forming a hard outer shell around the still-molten lava inside. The shell acts as insulation and keeps the internal lava in liquid form, enabling it to continue to flow. As the hot liquid drains away, it leaves behind a tunnel called a lava tube. Some lava tubes continue to drain lava from somewhere else in the volcano, while others are dry and empty. In Hawaii, you can find the longest and most extensive lava tubes.

Glacier Caves

The coldest place for a cave to form is within the frigid mass of a glacier. A glacier is a river of ice that flows very slowly over a long

period of time, accumulating snow in winter that then turns to ice. Gravity and the weight of the glacier make it slide downward along a thin layer of water below the mass of ice. This layer of water may have been caused by the pressure of the glacier moving over snow or from water that has seeped into cracks in the glacier through a

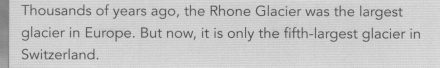

Thousands of years ago, the Rhone Glacier was the largest glacier in Europe. But now, it is only the fifth-largest glacier in Switzerland.

moulin—a deep shaft filled with melted water on the surface of a glacier. If you stand inside a glacier cave, you can see dark bands in the ice that indicate where ice has melted and refrozen. You can also see white lines that indicate winter snows. These bands can tell you what the climate was like during the history of the glacier.

Sea Caves

The final type of cave is a sea cave. Waves pummel the shores and cliffs of rocky coastlines, eroding soil and rock and carving out shallow caves from the base of the cliffs, creating huge overhangs. This process can take thousands of years. Despite the

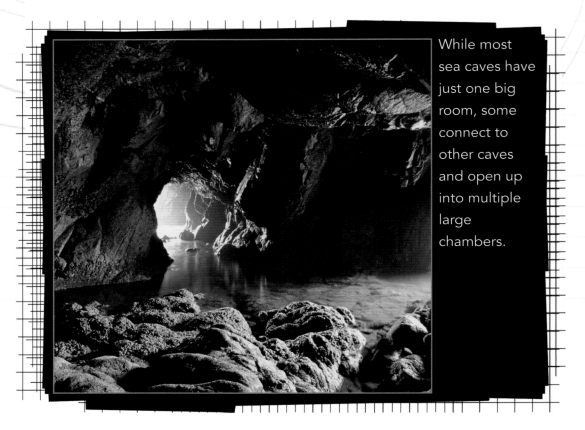

While most sea caves have just one big room, some connect to other caves and open up into multiple large chambers.

noise and fury of the sea outside, many sea caves are surprisingly quiet and calm inside. They contain still pools of water that are filled with all kinds of marine life, such as crabs and starfish, and even seals and sea lions, which use the caves as refuge during their journeys. Sea caves usually occur in sandstone but can also be found in limestone.

WHAT GROWS IN A CAVE?

As you walk through a limestone cave, you may hear dripping noises. And all around you are some very unusual formations—twisting columns, delicate fans, round and glowing pearls, white waves that resemble frosting on a cake. They're not plants, but they have grown in many caves for thousands of years. And they are just a few of the wondrous sights you can discover in limestone caves.

Cave Formations

Once a cave has been hollowed out by water, minerals in the remaining water and the atmospheric conditions in the cave lead to the creation of secondary formations called speleothems. As long as a cave continues to receive water and make cave formations, it is considered a live cave. Once a cave is dry and no water is entering it anymore, it is called a dead cave.

Stalactites

Small trickles of water run along cracks in a cave's ceiling. This water contains calcite, or calcium carbonate, which is the chemical that makes up limestone. Where a crack opens

One of the world's tallest columns is the Monarch, found in Slaughter Canyon Cave in Carlsbad Caverns National Park in New Mexico. It's 89 feet (27 meters) tall!

into the cave, a drop of dissolved limestone forms. As the drop hovers in the air, it releases some carbon dioxide and loses some limestone, creating a ring of dripstone around the drop. Eventually, the drop falls and the dripstone remains behind.

Over many thousands of years, the dripstone grows until it forms a long, thin, hollow tube, known as a soda straw stalactite. Soda straws are extremely fragile and sometimes break off on their own if they get too heavy. Conical stalactites form when the soda straw becomes filled with dripstone and water runs down the sides of the stalactite instead. The water leaves more dripstone at the top of the stalactite rather than at the bottom, giving it a conical shape.

Stalactites don't all grow at the same rate. If the ground above the cave is extremely fertile, with lots of trees and carbon dioxide, the water that passes through this ground will be more acidic. The more acidic the water is, the faster it will dissolve limestone, and the faster a stalactite will form. Usually, stalactites grow about a half inch (1.27 centimeters) to an inch (2.54 cm) every century. The Great Stalactite in Doolin Cave, Ireland, is more than 20 feet (6 meters) long!

Helectites

Helectites are similar to soda straws, but instead of growing straight down, they twist and curl in many directions, even back up toward the ceiling! One theory is that air currents and change in temperature cause these variations. Another theory is that the water has been forced through very tiny openings in the ceilings, walls, or floor. Helectites can also gather together and form large bushes that grow from the cave floor.

SEISMIC STALAGMITES!

Did you know that scientists are using stalagmites to learn more about earthquakes? Caverns in the Midwestern states of Illinois, Indiana, and Missouri contain stalagmites that formed around 195 years ago, the same time that the tremors of massive earthquakes may have fractured the rocks around the caves. Mineral-rich water flowed into the cracks and formed new stalagmites. By studying these formations, and others that have grown more recently, scientists may be able to learn more about how these earthquakes happened and what effect they have had on the landscape.

Stalagmites

When the drop of water that had been on the ceiling falls to the floor of the cave, it splashes, sending tiny droplets flying. The droplets lose more carbon dioxide and form more dripstone when they land. As more and more drops land in the same place, stalagmites form, growing with rounded tips back up toward the ceiling. Some stalagmites, called totem poles, grow to be tall and skinny. But some grow to be as big as skyscrapers and as wide as redwood trees.

An easy way to remember the difference between a stalactite and a stalagmite is that the "c" in stalactite refers to the ceiling of a cave, and the "g" in "stalagmite refers to the ground of a cave.

Sometimes, a stalagmite grows directly under a stalactite. When they meet, they form one solid structure called a column. It

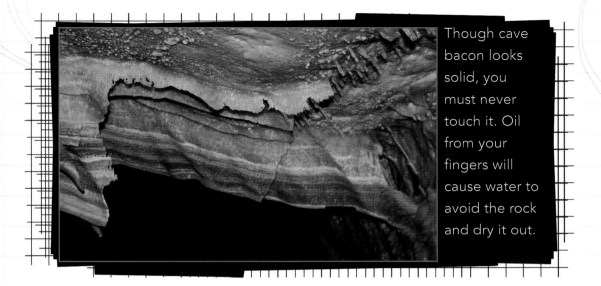

Though cave bacon looks solid, you must never touch it. Oil from your fingers will cause water to avoid the rock and dry it out.

can take hundreds of thousands of years for a column to form, and it can continue to grow as the water continues to drip and leave calcite behind.

Flowstone

In certain places, water flows down in thin sheets, creating draperies and curtains that seem to hang effortlessly from cave walls and ceilings. These sheets of water contain calcite and other cave minerals that are left behind as the water loses its carbon dioxide. Layers of these sheets form flowstone. Some of these curtains have bands of light and dark brown in them, giving them the name "cave bacon." Some curtains are translucent, meaning that light can pass through them, but they have a color of their own. In a vertical shaft, you can find flowstone formations that appear to be solid waterfalls.

Rimstone

Caves can have pools of excess water from the surface of the cave. The water in these pools contains many minerals. As the water moves, it causes calcite to collect around the edges of the pools. Eventually, the calcite forms dams called rimstones. Rimstone dams usually form on a slope, and the calcite flows over the edge of the pool. Rimstone is a very common cave formation.

Cave Pearls

A rare underwater cave decoration is the cave pearl. Similar to regular pearls, cave pearls start when a speck of dirt or other debris is coated with calcite in a pool. The speck floats on the surface of the pool and is rotated by the movement of the water. As the water ripples, calcite is added in layers around the speck. Eventually, the cave pearl becomes so big that it cannot float freely anymore, and it attaches to the side of the pool.

Popcorn, Shelfstone, and Frostwork

Sometimes, calcite balls cluster on cave walls, formed from splattered droplets of calcite that have fallen from the ceiling. These groups are called grapes or popcorn.

Another formation that forms on a cave pool is shelfstone. Shelfstone begins as a very thin floating calcite raft. Eventually, the raft attaches itself to a rock wall at one side of the pool. Years of mineral deposits thicken the raft into a shelf.

In some caves, the limestone dissolves into aragonite instead of calcite. Aragonite is made from the same chemical as calcite,

Some caves have several nests of cave pearls, which can be as big as golf balls or as tiny as grains of salt.

but with a slightly different structure. This creates a completely different sort of formation, called frostwork, that is pointy and resembles a thorny white flower. Frostwork can sometimes grow over other formations, such as cave popcorn.

Gypsum

Limestone caves formed by sulfuric acid have their own unique crystals and mineral formations. Some are made from a mineral called gypsum, which is a soft form of calcite. Gypsum formations are often branching structures that look like flowers or chandeliers.

Others are simply single crystals that can grow quite tall. In Naica Cave in Mexico, some gypsum crystals were measured at more than 30 feet (9 m) long and 3 feet (1 m) wide!

Snotites

Another sulfur cave decoration is called a snotite because of its resemblance to mucus escaping from a runny nose. Drops of sulfuric acid, highly dangerous to human skin, form on the ceiling

24

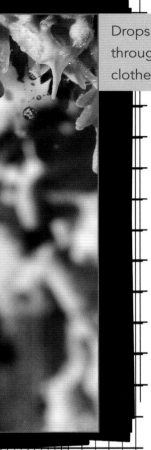

Drops of sulfuric acid in these snotite formations can burn through clothing and harm skin. Cavers wear masks and special clothes to stay safe.

and grow down to the floor of the cave, similar to stalactites. Extremophiles, microscopic bacteria, live off of the sulfuric acid.

Since most speleothems are made of calcite, aragonite, or gypsum, they are usually white. However, from time to time, certain impurities are introduced into the calcite, and reddish or brownish hues may be present.

Moonmilk

The last cave decoration we will look at is called moonmilk. It is a white cheese-like substance that, when wet, is similar to other formations in their early stages, except that it does not become hard like stone. It is formed in limestone caves from calcite and other materials. And it is made up of more than 50 percent water. Scientists believe that moonmilk contains bacteria that help it grow by eating away at minerals in the cave walls and adding to the moonmilk.

Many of the cave decorations have funny names and unusual appearances. But all are fragile and have taken thousands of years to form. It is very important that cavers, people who explore caves, move slowly and carefully to avoid damaging these decorations. We'll talk more about cave exploration and safety in chapter five.

CHAPTER 3

LIFE IN CAVES

All kinds of animals choose to live in these dark, damp shelters. Some of them may be familiar, but others are so unusual that chances are you have never heard of or seen them before. When you think of the kinds of animals that live in caves, you probably first think of bats. But there are many other, more unusual animals that live in caves. Caves have three main ecosystems, called zones, and they change dramatically as you move farther into a cave.

Cave Zones

The first zone is called the epigean zone. It is also known as the entrance zone. It's the smallest of all the ecosystems and is located at the front of the cave. This zone has a similar climate to the outdoors and receives lots of sunlight during the day, though the roof of the cave keeps this area a bit cooler than the outside temperature. The animals that live in the entrance zone are called trogloxenes, or "cave visitors," because they occasionally visit the cave and stay for a bit, and then leave. They are the only ones that leave the cave to reproduce. Some of these animals include raccoons, pack rats, snakes, bears, and porcupines.

Throughout Bandhavgarh National Park in India, you can often find Bengal tigers escaping the daytime heat in the cool shade of a cave.

The second cave zone is called the endogean, or twilight, zone. It encompasses the area just behind the entrance of the cave. While it still receives some sunlight, it is darker and cooler, even in the summer, than the entrance zone. The animals that live here are called troglophiles, or "cave lovers," because, though they can live elsewhere—and sometimes leave to do so—they often spend their whole lives in this section of the cave.

Bats are considered important troglophiles, since they spend so much of their time in the cave. We'll learn more about bats a little later in this chapter. Animals who live in this zone, such as owls and bats, frequently sleep in the cave and leave to hunt. Other animals include earthworms, cave crickets, beetles, and salamanders.

The third cave zone is the most unusual. Called the trypogean, or "dark," zone, it has absolutely no light at all. Here, the cave takes on the temperature of the surrounding rocks. It's cool and wet year-round. Shrouded in complete darkness, lost in a maze of passageways, the animals who live here are called troglobites, or "cave dwellers," and they cannot live anywhere else. Examples of these animals include blind crayfish, giant cave centipedes, eyeless shrimp, glowworms, and spiders that do not spin webs. There are more than seven thousand known species of troglobites, but since they're so good at hiding, and there are still so many caves to explore, no one knows yet how many total species there are in these dark zones.

Unusual Creatures

Troglobites are primitive, and many have no eyes. They have lived in total darkness for so long that they no longer have any use for the sense of sight. Their other senses, however, are sharply acute. The blind salamander has sensory organs along its body that can detect tiny movements in water. It uses these organs to find its prey. Troglobites have also adapted their bodies to handle the rough terrain of dark zones, growing long legs with spiky feet, long antennae, and a white or even translucent body color, as they have no need for coloration or camouflage.

The biggest challenge these troglobites face is finding a steady source of food. They must be willing to eat anything that is available. Their populations are very small, their physical size is small, and they are almost always near starvation. It's not an easy existence.

The Texas blind salamander is an endangered species whose survival is threatened by groundwater pollution.

In every zone, the source of food comes from outside. But dwellers, who cannot leave the cave, must depend completely on visitors or underground streams that flow from outside the cave for food.

Food can come in many forms: bugs and insects that wander into the back of the cave or are carried in by other animals; seeds and plant material that are also carried in; animals that grow sick and die; or bat droppings, called guano. Some troglobites can live for weeks, even months, without eating. Their bodies have adapted to survive on very little food for a very long time—some with life spans of more than a hundred years.

Glowworm Genius

One troglobite species has devised a unique way to catch its food. In New Zealand's Waitomo Caves, glowworms have special mucous glands in their mouths that make silk. They lower long wet strands like shining fishing lines from the ceiling of the cave.

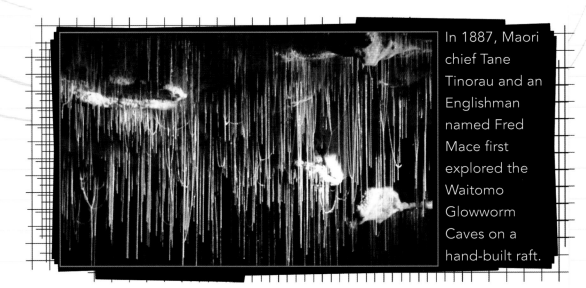

In 1887, Maori chief Tane Tinorau and an Englishman named Fred Mace first explored the Waitomo Glowworm Caves on a hand-built raft.

After setting dozens of them, a glowworm inches back up to its nest and waits. In the darkness, the hind end of the glowworm glows blue from a chemical reaction inside the worm. The light acts as a lure, a temptation to unsuspecting insects flying by. Once stuck in a sticky strand, the insect can only struggle and sway—there is no escape. The glowworm lowers itself down the line and eats its prey live. By setting so many lines, the glowworm ensures a steady supply of food.

Scientists think that most ground troglobites are descendants of troglophiles that ventured toward the back of the cave and never returned to the entrance. Perhaps they liked the cooler conditions or the climate at the front of the cave was too forbidding. It's still a mystery as to when this transition happened.

Bats!

Now, let's take a look at those important troglophiles—bats. Long associated with the mystery and terror of caves and dark spaces,

HUNGRY FOR SOME SOUP?

Like bats, swiftlets are cave lovers, but they hunt during the day and roost at night. These elusive birds are found in caves in southern Asia, the islands of the South Pacific, and northeastern Australia. They live very high up in these caves, away from predators, in nests they have built entirely of saliva. The saliva acts as a glue so that the nests can stick to the cave walls. The nests are not more than 1 inch (2.54 cm) wide, and each one takes about thirty days to build.

With such tiny homes to return to, how do swiftlets find their way? Scientists think they use the same method that bats do: echolocation. The birds send out clicks and listen to their echoes to locate their nests. The exact process is still a mystery.

Swiftlets' nests are the main ingredient in a Chinese delicacy called bird's nest soup. But harvesting these nests is a dangerous undertaking. Gatherers must climb extremely long rope ladders that sway in the wind. As a result, the nests and soup are very expensive.

bats are actually a key species in the ecosystem of a cave. There are more than 1,100 species of bats in the world. Their guano provides food for a variety of creatures, including cockroaches. The cockroaches, in turn, become food for giant centipedes. Crabs also burrow through the bat droppings for nutrients.

Many species of bats perch on the ceilings of caves, resting there during the day and tending to their young. When twilight comes, they leave the cave in a whirling black mass, taking to the skies in search of a meal. Bats can eat more than half their body weight in insects each night. But they often encounter danger.

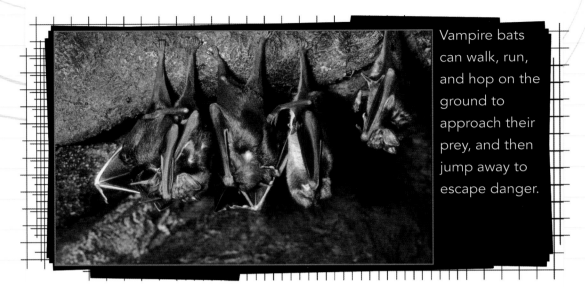

Vampire bats can walk, run, and hop on the ground to approach their prey, and then jump away to escape danger.

Peregrine falcons and bat hawks are also out hunting at twilight, and they are on the lookout for a bat to leave the group. Those that do return to the cave find their way using echolocation—they send out a call and listen for the call to come back. They use the echoes to judge the distance and size of the objects in their path. Though bats are not blind at all, their sonar is a reliable way for them to navigate in the dark.

In the United States, most bats do not migrate to warmer climates in the winter. Instead, they hibernate at the back of caves in the dark zones. They hang from the ceilings and walls and do not eat until spring, protected by the constant cool temperature and isolation. They have just enough food reserves to carry them through the long sleep. However, if they are awakened in the middle of their hibernation, they risk starvation and death. The energy they burn waking up and returning to sleep uses up some of their reserve. They may not be able to last until spring.

CAVES AROUND THE WORLD

Caves must have seemed inhospitable, with wild animals lurking outside and a cold, damp atmosphere inside. However, many early people did live in caves, as early as a million years ago and as recently as tens of thousands of years ago, during the last glacial period. Evidence of ancient cave communities has been found throughout Asia and Europe. Archaeologists have learned about these people from the fossils and tools they left behind. In some cases, the same caves were used over and over again, and archaeologists have uncovered layers of litter.

These caves provided refuge, especially during the glacial period. People built fires to scare away wild animals, to cook food, and to stay warm. But these people didn't spend all their time hunting and trying to survive. They used caves for other, more creative activities.

Cave Paintings

Among the most famous of the painted caves is Lascaux, in central France. The Lascaux cave was created during the Paleolithic period, which spans from 2.5 million years ago to about 10,000 years ago. This period includes the

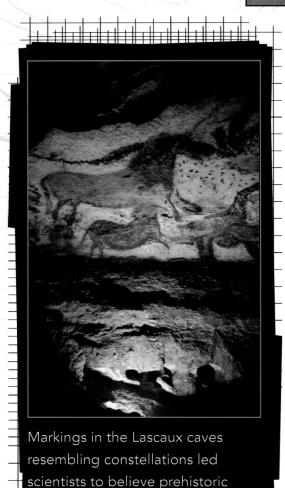

Markings in the Lascaux caves resembling constellations led scientists to believe prehistoric humans knew of star formations.

development of stone tools and the beginnings of art and religious rituals.

In Lascaux, on September 12, 1940, four boys stumbled onto the entrance of a cave that hid a great museum inside. On the walls of the cave were prehistoric paintings, perfectly preserved, that depicted bulls, horses, and aurochs—a species of large cattle that had become extinct in the 1600s. As the boys crept farther into the cave, they found more painted rooms. These rooms are now called the Great Hall of the Bulls, the Lateral Passage, the Shaft of the Dead Man, the Chamber of Engravings, the Painted Gallery, and the Chamber of Felines. The paintings have been dated to around sixteen thousand years ago. The cave was opened to the public after World War II, but the presence of so many people every day began to damage the paintings. The cave was then closed to the public, and a replica was constructed so that people could continue to see the images.

To create these works of art, the Paleolithic people used minerals they found in the cave—iron oxide and manganese for red, gray, brown, and purple; calcite for white; and charred wood for black. They ground the minerals into powders and placed them in hollowed bones. For brushes, they used pads of fur or their fingers. Sometimes they drew with charcoal first and then filled in the outlines with paint. They burned animal fat to shed light on their stone canvasses.

Altamira

The paintings at Lascaux were not the first cave paintings to be discovered. In Spain, in 1879, a man named Marcelino Sanz de Sautuola and his daughter, Maria, were digging in a cave in Altamira meadow looking for prehistoric objects when Maria wandered away, deep into the cave. Suddenly, she shouted for her father. Together, they stared at huge paintings of bison, deer, wild boar, and horses on the walls and ceiling of the chamber. The animals were depicted in hues of red and gray, with black outlines. These were the same animals whose bones Marcelino had found elsewhere in the cave.

Excited, Marcelino began to tell people about the Paleolithic artwork. But no one believed that such a primitive culture could have created these beautiful paintings. The colors were also too well preserved, they thought, to be so old. The paintings were thought to be fakes until, many years later, the Paleolithic caves in France were discovered. At last, Marcelino Sautuola was proven correct, long after his death.

Tassili

Located in Algeria, the Tassili N'Ajjer mountain range in the Sahara Desert seems like an odd place to find cave artwork. However,

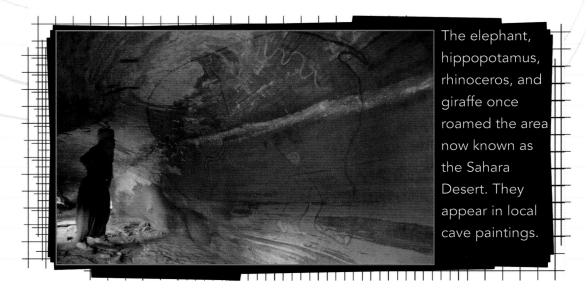

The elephant, hippopotamus, rhinoceros, and giraffe once roamed the area now known as the Sahara Desert. They appear in local cave paintings.

several thousand years ago, the Sahara was not a desert but a lush, fertile land. Throughout this region are caves full of paintings and engravings that chronicle the events in the lives of the people, the changes in climate, and the movements of animal herds from about 8,000 to about 1,500 years ago. There are more than fifteen thousand works of art in Tassili, and they are significant because their images feature humans engaging in daily activities, unlike the cave paintings in Europe, which almost exclusively depict animals.

Cappadocia

Cappadocia, Turkey, has an otherworldly landscape full of stone caves that are still used as homes today. The rocks are shades of tan or pink or white, and they change color with the movement of the sun. The structures have many shapes—towers, spires, cones, and castles. And they have sheltered all kinds of people from early Christians during the first centuries CE, through the early 1800s, when Turks were escaping from the Egyptian army.

These rock formations were created from deposits caused by volcanic eruptions that occurred millions of years ago. These deposits of lava were pounded and pummeled by rain and snow, earthquakes and rivers, until they became a substance called tuff—a soft rock.

From this material, people constructed homes, monasteries, and churches. And in these churches are collections of cave paintings of a different sort. Beautiful paintings of Christian symbols and icons adorn these walls. The style of artwork is called Byzantine, named after the Byzantine Empire that ruled

Many of the cave homes in Cappadocia are quite nice inside, with fancy carpets and stone furniture and bathrooms.

this part of the world, where Turkey is now located. These paintings can be dated as far back as the seventh century on up through the thirteenth century.

The best-known monuments in Cappadocia are the "fairy chimneys"—tall cones of tuff with caps of hard rock on top. The cap protects the soft rock underneath from erosion and weather. Cappadocia's other secret is several underground cities with dangerous traps and heavy stone doors that were also used for refuge.

Incredible Caves

All around the world are caves that stand out for their size, their inhabitants, their history, or their beauty. Some of these caves have folktales about spirits and mythological creatures that once inhabited them. Others have tall tales about how they were discovered. And some just take your breath away when you step inside and hold up your flashlight. Let's look at five unique caves that have inspired explorers and visitors for decades.

Blue Grotto

The Blue Grotto is a sea cave on the coast of the island of Capri. The interior of the cave is a luminous blue, caused by sunlight that penetrates an underwater chamber and shines up through the surface of the water. The Blue Grotto is the emblem of the island of Capri and a popular tourist destination. It was once known as Gradola, after the nearby town, but superstitious stories forced the name to be changed to the Blue Grotto. The cave was used long ago as a monument to nymphs and sea gods, and there were statues of these mythological figures inside the cave. The statues have since been moved to a museum.

Sarawak Chamber

Deep in the forests of Gunung Mulu National Park, in Malaysia, is Sarawak Chamber. At 2,297 feet (700 m) long, this gigantic

EXTREME CAVES

Longest cave system	Mammoth Cave system, USA	345 miles (555 km)
Longest under-water cave	Nohoch Nah Chich, Mexico	24.5 miles (39.4 km)
Longest lava tube	Kazamura, Hawaii	16 miles (25.7 km)
Biggest cave chamber	Sarawak Chamber, Malaysia	2,297 feet (700 m) long
Tallest stalagmite	Krasnohorska, Slovakia	105 feet (32 m)
Longest stalactite	Cueva de Nerja, Spain	194 feet (59 m)

room could easily fit several jumbo jets! The chamber was first discovered in January 1981 by three Englishmen—Andy Eavis, Dave Checkley, and Tony White, all very experienced cave explorers. They had been hiking through the mountainous jungle of the park when they found a river passage. The river led them to an underground chamber so huge and so dark that their head lamps were of no use. The men had found Sarawak Chamber. It ranges in width from 656 feet (200 m) to 1,410 feet (430 m) at its widest point, and it is around 328 feet (100 m) high.

Mammoth Cave

With more than 350 miles (563 km) of known passageways, Mammoth Cave—located in the state of Kentucky—is the world's longest cave system. The first people to discover Mammoth Cave were early Native Americans, about four thousand years ago. Scientists have found many artifacts in the cave, such as moccasins and bowls made out of hollowed gourds. Scientists believe Native Americans lived in this cave and used its minerals as ritual body paint, medicine, and food spices.

European settlers found Mammoth Cave much later. There is a story that around the start of the nineteenth century, a man named James Hutchins was hunting one day and followed a wounded black bear to the entrance of a cave. Though it is unclear whether or not he managed to kill the bear, he was the first European to set foot inside Mammoth Cave.

Settlers first used Mammoth Cave to mine saltpeter during the War of 1812. Saltpeter is another name for potassium nitrate—an important ingredient in gunpowder—and it is found in the bat guano that collects on the floor of the cave. It is thought that some two hundred tons of saltpeter were mined during this time.

After the war ended, the cave was turned into a tourist destination, and then a tuberculosis sanitarium. A doctor named John Croghan believed that the air in the cave could cure his patients. Unfortunately, the cold, damp air had the opposite effect. Not only did his patients die but he, too, died from tuberculosis.

Two famous cave explorers greatly contributed to the knowledge we have today about Mammoth Cave's passageways. In 1839, a

Dr. John Croghan's hospital was located more than 160 feet (48 m) underground, deep inside Mammoth Cave. Mammoth Cave is located in the state of Kentucky.

young slave named Stephen Bishop became the new tour guide for Mammoth Cave. Bishop was knowledgeable and likeable, and people enjoyed his tours. He was allowed to explore the cave, and he was the first to cross a deep canyon, called the Bottomless Pit, to discover two new rivers and see an eyeless fish—an unusual troglobite living in the rivers' waters.

In 1925, a man named Floyd Collins started exploring Sand Cave, an opening he hoped would connect his cave—Crystal Cave—with the immensely popular Mammoth Cave and bring him money and fame. Unfortunately, the cave collapsed on him. After about eighteen days of rescue efforts, he was found, but he had died about three days prior. He did bring fame to Crystal Cave, however. It was renamed Floyd Collins' Crystal Cave.

Carlsbad Caverns

At the beginning of the twentieth century, a cowboy named Jim White saw something unusual in the skies over the Guadalupe foothills of New Mexico Territory. What looked like a black funnel cloud seemed to be hovering in the air, not far away. Intrigued, he went to see what this cloud could be and where it was coming from. His curiosity led him to the entrance to a cavern on a hillside, out of which were swarming thousands of small brown bats. As White explored the cave over the next two decades, he entered enormous chambers and saw cave formations that were both majestic and delicate. But no one believed his tales. Such an ordinary hillside couldn't possibly hide such magical splendor. In 1922, a photographer accompanied White and captured the cave's secrets on film, and after that the world flocked to see White's caves and the bats swarm and swoop every evening. Carlsbad Caverns is now a national park and is recognized as one of the most beautiful caverns in the world. Its sulfur-based formations and huge chambers are astounding. Another cave in the park, Lechuguilla Cave, is one of the deepest caves in the world and is famous for its incredible rock formations.

CAVING AND EXPLORATION

I n the world of cave exploration, there are show caves and wild caves. Show caves are developed—they have artificial lighting, staircases, elevators, and sights to see at every step. People pay money to see show caves and expect to be entertained.

But wild caves are just that—wild. They are not developed. They don't have any technology inside. They remain the way nature created them—dark and wet, and full of obstacles, pitfalls, and wrong turns. They should only be explored by an experienced caver.

The Sport of Caving

Caving, also called spelunking, is the sport of exploring caves. It carries with it the thrills of danger and new discoveries, the aura and allure of an extreme adventure. Cavers explore frozen glaciers, dive down into dark underwater passageways, step gingerly into inky black nooks crawling with unknown insects, and wriggle through impossibly tight spaces, all in search of something unexpected and new.

Caving and speleology were started by a Frenchman named Edouard-Alfred Martel. He was the first to examine

You never know what acrobatic moves you might need as you move through a cave, so it's important to be alert and prepared.

and study caves from a scientific perspective. He explored thousands of caves in his home country of France and elsewhere in the world, giving legitimacy to the sport of caving and the science of cave study and knowledge. He also founded the Société de Spéléologie, the first organization focused on the study of caves.

As with any sport, caving has its dangers. Caves are full of dead ends, narrow openings called "squeezes," unsteady rocks, and breakdowns where rocks have fallen in from the ceiling. Experienced cavers learn techniques that help them navigate these uncertainties. They also have cave maps, which we'll look at a little later in this chapter.

Exploring Underwater Caves

Cave diving, as underwater cave exploring is called, can be thrilling. Divers slip into a watery blue realm where noise and light are gone and eerie columns and spindly needles point the way to shadowy tunnels.

But the dangers are serious. Cave diving is not like diving in a swimming pool. You cannot always exit straight up. You may have to swim horizontally for a long time. You must set a turnaround time so that you have enough air for the return trip, plus some extra in case something goes wrong.

Underwater cave ceilings are not always stable and could crumble at any time, causing injury or blocking your way out.

Tight spaces can present two potential dangers. Equipment may not fit through a narrow crevice, and squeezing through such a tight space can cause a silt-out, in which the silt or soil on the sea floor gets mixed in the water, making it impossible to see. A diver can become disoriented in a silt-out and lose all sense of direction.

Cave divers go through training and certification to learn how to handle the dangers and dive safely. There are two kinds of certifications: cavern diving and cave diving. Cavern diving allows you to dive into a cave as long as you can still see the entrance. Once you can no longer see your way out, you must turn around.

Cave diving, on the other hand, is much more technical. This certification teaches you how to lay a dive line, how to exit a completely dark cave with no light, good diving techniques, and many other things. A dive line is a spool of nylon cord. It is tied to a rock at the entrance and then unspooled as the diver enters the cave. The diver relies on the dive line to find the exit to the cave and to stay balanced and upright in a silt-out. Some dive lines have measurements on them that a diver can use to measure distances during the trip. These measurements will help the diver map the cave.

A cave diver uses the following equipment, with backups of everything:

A black mask that absorbs light so that the diver can focus on what's in front of him or her.

In Mexico, there are more than three thousand cenotes (say-NOH-tays), or sinkholes, that were once the only source of freshwater for the ancient Mayan people.

A hood to keep the head safe during dives.

Lightweight, stiff fins to avoid big kicks that could cause silt-outs.

Either a dry suit or a wet suit, depending on the kind of dive. A dry suit keeps the body dry and warm and is often used when entering extremely cold or icy water.

Gadgets like flashlights, knives, air gauges, and compasses that all fit together to make them easier to carry.

Air tanks. To avoid "the bends," as decompression sickness is often called, a diver must return to the surface slowly to allow his or her body to adjust to the changes in pressure. With proper training, a diver can learn the correct amount of air to use at each level to surface safely.

Cartography

Cartography is the study of maps and mapmaking. Cavers and cave divers use maps to navigate through known passageways

COMMON RULES TO FOLLOW WHEN CAVING

Never enter a cave by yourself. Always bring at least two other experienced cavers with you in case of emergency, and stay together. Know your abilities and don't explore caves that are too difficult for you.

- Tell someone where you are going and when you think you'll be back.
- Make sure you have all the necessary equipment.
- Wear strong, sturdy clothing and shoes.
- Wear a good helmet with a chin strap.
- Have a good light source and two backups in case the batteries run out. A helmet light is recommended.
- Bring extra food. A caving expedition may take longer than you expect.
- Take along a heat source, such as a candle or a stove.
- Bring a first-aid kit.
- Carry out all your trash.
- Make no permanent marks. Use plastic flags that you can pick up on your way out of the cave.
- Stay on the path to avoid damaging any wildlife.
- Have an emergency plan and discuss it with your team.

It's important that you follow these instructions as well as any additional information your guides may give you. If you are going to explore glacier caves, lava caves, or sea caves, there may be different, more specific sets of instructions. Understand them thoroughly beforehand.

and discover new ones. Experienced cavers are observant and pay attention to directional changes, elevation changes, and landmarks. They stop and look at where they've been and where they are going when passageways split, and they commit that information to memory. It's their ticket to making it out of the cave safely.

The next step is to draw the cave and re-create the distances, formations, and twists. This is much more difficult because steps taken underground may not be the same size as steps taken above ground, not to mention the distances covered by wriggling through crevices. Cavers must look at rock formations and fault lines to understand and then convey the topography, or layout, of the cave in a map.

Cave cartographers use three main tools: a compass, a clinometer (which measures incline), and a measuring tape. As cavers navigate passageways, they make measurements along the way that then help them sketch the interior of the cave.

Protecting Caves and Cave Formations

While caving is an exciting sport, it is important to also be mindful that caves are a part of nature and must be treated with care.

One hot debate among cavers today is whether or not to reveal cave locations to the public. On the one hand, an informed citizen can effectively advocate for the preservation and upkeep of a local cave. On the other hand, too much publicity could result in too many expeditions by too many novice cavers, leading to dirty and damaged caves.

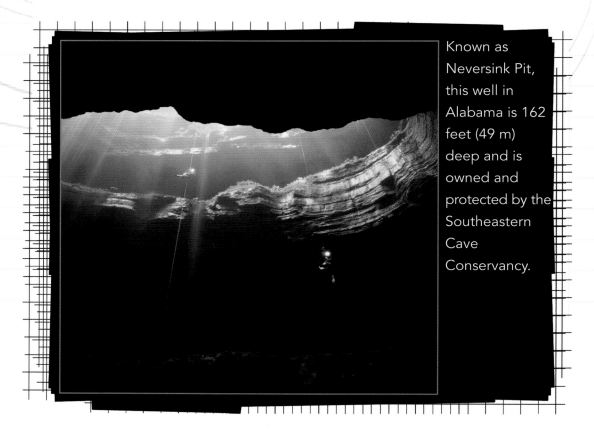

Known as Neversink Pit, this well in Alabama is 162 feet (49 m) deep and is owned and protected by the Southeastern Cave Conservancy.

The speleothems inside limestone caves are thousands upon thousands of years old. One swipe of the arm or one misplaced step could erase all that time and energy and growth, not to mention beauty. Experienced cavers practice careful movements before entering caves by setting up obstacle courses and trying various maneuvers until they find one that is the least likely to cause any damage.

The area around a cave can also be harmed. Many caves are on private property. Landowners would rather not have herds of people cross their fields and land, bothering animals and risking injury. As a result, there is a complex process involved in getting permission to explore these private caves to reduce the number of people trampling on private land. An important second caving motto is: "Cave softly." Don't do anything that would permanently alter a cave in any way.

Future of Cave Exploration

Caving is an ever-evolving activity. New technology makes it possible to explore farther, deeper, lower, and higher than ever before.

Researchers in Colorado are developing a way to find caves using heat sensors, a technology called thermal remote sensing imagery. The hope is that if this procedure works on Earth, it might help scientists locate caves on Mars.

In Florida's Wakulla Springs, an expedition called the Wakulla 2 will use a digital wall mapper (DWM) as well as other equipment to create the world's first three-dimensional digital map of an underwater cave. The DWM uses eight computers and sonar (a technology similar to the echolocation used by bats) to plot the contours of the cave. This new kind of map will enable potential divers to explore the cave ahead of time and avoid dangers. And scientists can monitor any cave damage caused by changes in climate and pollution.

There are thousands of caves just waiting to be explored. They might be in the hottest or coldest parts of the earth. They might contain a new troglobite species. They might have a new kind of cave formation. They could even be in your hometown. Use the information at the end of this book to find caves in your area and learn more about them. Become a "soft caver" and help preserve these incredible geological wonders hidden away deep inside our planet.

GLOSSARY

calcite A mineral that forms from dissolved limestone, chalk, and marble.

cartography The study of maps and mapmaking.

cave A natural opening to an underground chamber or series of chambers.

caving The sport of exploring caves; also called spelunking.

dive line A nylon cord used by cave divers to aid navigation and measurement.

erosion The destructive effect of weather or acid on a substance like rock or ice.

extremophile A tiny organism that can live in extreme conditions.

glacier A large body of ice that slowly moves down a mountain slope or valley.

guano Fertilizer containing droppings of birds or bats.

hydrogen sulfide A poisonous gas that contains sulfur and has the smell of rotting eggs.

karst A limestone area with sinkholes, underground streams, and caverns.

limestone A rock made from the remains of shells and marine animals that is used in building.

moulin A vertical shaft of melted ice water in a glacier.

Paleolithic Term used to describe the early part of the Stone Age.

phreatic Term used to describe a cave that is created in water-filled passages.

sandstone Sedimentary rock that is made from sand.

sedimentary Rock that is formed from deposits of debris by wind or water.

shaft A long, vertical opening to a cave.

speleology   Scientific study or exploration of caves.

speleothems Cave formations that grow after a cave has formed.

stalactite An icicle of calcite that hangs from the ceiling of a cave.

stalagmite A tower of calcite that grows from the floor of a cave.

troglobite A type of unusual animal that lives in the back of a cave for its entire life.

troglophile An animal, such as a bat or cave swiftlet, that roosts in a cave and hunts outside the cave.

trogloxene An animal that occasionally stays in the entrance of a cave.

water table The upper limit of the water level in a flooded cave.

FOR MORE INFORMATION

American Cave Conservation Association
119 East Main Street
P.O. Box 409
Horse Cave, KY 42749
(270) 786-1466
E-mail: acca@cavern.org
Web site: http://www.cavern.org
The ACCA educates people about caves and karstlands to promote the conservation of caves and related resources.

Canadian Cave Conservancy
P.O. Box 8124
Sta Central P.O.
Victoria, BC V8W 2Y2
Canada
E-mail: canadiancaveconservancy@shaw.ca
Web site: http://www.cancaver.ca/CCC
The CCA's purpose is to further the conservation of cave and karst resources in Canada.

Cave Research Foundation
6304 Kaybro Street
Laurel, MD 20707
E-mail: pnkambesis@juno.com

Web site: http://www.cave-research.org
The CRF promotes exploration and documentation of caves and karst areas, supports research, aids in conservation, and educates the public.

National Speleological Society

2813 Cave Avenue
Huntsville, AL 3580-4431
(256) 852-1300
E-mail: nss@caves.org
Web site: http://www.caves.org
The NSS studies, explores, and conserves cave and karst resources.

Southeastern Cave Conservancy, Inc.

P. O. Box 71857
Chattanooga, TN 37407-0857
(615) 566-5129
E-mail: info@scci.org
Web site: http://www.scci.org
The SCCI is dedicated to regional cave conservation, caver education, and cave management.

Toronto Caving Group

1116 Wilson Avenue
P.O. Box 66129
Toronto, ON M3M 1G7
Canada
(647) 892-5240
E-mail: kirkm@globalserve.net
Web site: http://www.orbonline.net/~tcg

The Toronto Caving Group is one of the oldest continuously active caving clubs in Canada and the largest caving club in Ontario. It organizes events and teaches techniques.

Web Sites

Due to the changing nature of Internet links, Rosen Publishing has developed an online list of Web sites related to the subject of this book. This site is updated regularly. Please use this link to access the list:

http://www.rosenlinks.com/lan/cave

FOR FURTHER READING

Burger, Paul. *Cave Exploring: The Definitive Guide to Caving Technique, Safety, Gear, and Trip Leadership.* Guilford, CT: Falcon Guides, 2006.

Culver, David C., and William B. White, eds. *Encyclopedia of Caves.* Burlington, MA: Academic Press, 2004.

Friend, Sandra. *Sinkholes.* Sarasota, FL: Pineapple Press, 2002.

Howes, Chris. *Radical Sports: Caving.* Chicago, IL: Heinemann, 2003.

Rea, G. Thomas, ed. *Caving Basics: A Comprehensive Guide for Beginning Cavers.* Huntsville, AL: National Speleological Society, 1992.

Stone, William, Barbara am Ende, and Monte Paulsen. *Beyond the Deep: The Deadly Descent into the World's Most Treacherous Cave.* New York, NY: Warner Books, 2002.

Waltham, Tony. *Great Caves of the World.* Buffalo, NY: Firefly Books Ltd., 2008.

BIBLIOGRAPHY

Allman, Tony. *Life in a Cave*. Detroit, MI: Kidhaven Press, 2005.

Bendick, Jeanne. *Caves! Underground Worlds*. New York, NY: Henry Holt and Company, 1995.

Bio-Medicine. "Discovery of New Cave Millipedes Casts Light on Arizona Cave Ecology." Retrieved October 28, 2008 (http://www.bio-medicine.org/biology-news/Discovery-of-new-cave-millipedes-casts-light-on-Arizona-cave-ecology-5201-1).

Brucker, Roger W., and Richard A. Watson. *The Longest Cave*. New York, NY: Alfred A. Knopf, 1976.

Bunnell, Dave. "The Virtual Lava Tube." The Virtual Cave. Retrieved October 22, 2008 (http://www.goodearthgraphics.com/virtual_tube/virtube.html).

Doolin Cave. "History." Retrieved October 24, 2008 (http://www.doolincave.ie/history.htm).

Dougherty, P. H. "Caves and Karst of Kentucky." Kentucky Geological Survey. Retrieved October 21, 2008 (http://www.uky.edu/KGS/education/mammothcave.htm).

Duckeck, Jochen. "Edouard Alfred Martel." Showcaves. Retrieved October 27, 2008 (http://www.showcaves.com/english/explain/People/Martel.html).

Duckeck, Jochen. "Speleology." Showcaves. Retrieved October 22, 2008 (http://www.showcaves.com/english/explain/Speleology/index.html).

Ende, Barbara am. "Solving Wakulla Springs Underwater Mysteries." *Hydro International*. Retrieved October 28, 2008 (http://www.hydro-international.com/issues/ articles/id209-Solving_Wakulla_Springs_Underwater_ Mysteries.html).

Fuller, John. "How Cave Diving Works." How Stuff Works. Retrieved October 27, 2008 (http://adventure.howstuffworks. com/cave-diving.htm).

Fuller, John. "What's the Difference Between Stalactites and Stalagmites?" How Stuff Works. Retrieved October 24, 2008 (http://science.howstuffworks.com/stalactite-stalagmite.htm).

Harrison, David L. *The World of American Caves*. Chicago, IL: Reilly & Lee Books, 1970.

How Stuff Works. "All About Glaciers." Retrieved October 23, 2008 (http://www.howstuffworks.com/framed.htm?parent=question9. htm&url=http://nsidc.org/glaciers).

Kamm, Henry. "Cappodocia's Lunar Landscape." *New York Times*. Retrieved October 26, 2008 (http://query.nytimes.com/ gst/fullpage.html?sec=travel&res=9E06E3DE1638F934A15753 C1A963948260&fta=y).

Krajick, Kevin. "Discoveries in the Dark." National Geographic Society. Retrieved October 25, 2008 (http://ngm. nationalgeographic.com/2007/09/new-troglobites/ new-troglobites-text.html).

Kramer, Stephen. *Caves*. Minneapolis, MN: Carolrhoda Books, Inc., 1995.

MSN. "Cave." Retrieved October 23, 2008 (http://encarta.msn. com/encyclopedia_761561626/cave.html).

Museo de Altamira. "Discovery." Retrieved October 25, 2008 (http://museodealtamira.mcu.es/ingles/descubrimiento.html).

National Centre of Prehistory. "The Cave of Lascaux." Retrieved October 25, 2008 (http://www.culture.gouv.fr/culture/arcnat/lascaux/en).

National Geographic Society. "Caves." Retrieved October 23, 2008 (http://science.nationalgeographic.com/science/earth/surface-of-the-earth/caves-article.html).

National Park Service. "The Archaic Ones." Retrieved October 25, 2007 (https://cms.ser.nps.gov/maca/historyculture/history1.htm).

National Park Service. "Wind Cave National Park: Speleothems." Retrieved October 23, 2008 (http://www.nps.gov/archive/wica/Speleothems.htm).

PBS. "Borneo: Island in the Clouds." Retrieved October 21, 2008 (http://www.pbs.org/edens/borneo/mtcaves.htm).

PBS. "How Caves Form." Retrieved October 23, 2008 (http://www.pbs.org/wgbh/nova/caves/form.html).

Perkins, Sid. "Earthquake History Recorded in Stalagmites." Science News. Retrieved October 24, 2008 (http://www.sciencenews.org/view/generic/id/37262/title/Earthquake_history_recorded_in_stalagmites).

Planet Earth: The Complete BBC Series. Directed by Alastair Fothergill. 2006. London, England: 2 entertain, 2007.

Prior, Natalie Jane. Caves, Graves, and Catacombs: Secrets from Beneath the Earth. Chicago, IL: Allen & Unwin, 1996.

Regione Campania. "The Legend of the Blue Grotto." Retrieved October 27, 2008 (http://www.culturacampania.rai.it/site/en-GB/Cultural_Heritage/Archaelogical_areas_and_Nature_parks/Scheda/capri_grotta_azzurra.html?link=storia).

Roth, John. "Moonmilk and Cave-Dwelling Microbes." National Park Service. Retrieved October 25, 2008 (http://www.nps.gov/archive/crla/notes/vol26h.htm).

SERA Karst Task Force, Inc. "SERA Karst Task Force." Retrieved October 23, 2008 (http://sktfi.org).

Sherman, Sophia. "Waitamo: New Zealand's Glow-worm Caves." Nature Institute. Retrieved October 25, 2008 (http://www.natureinstitute.org/pub/ic/ic13/worms.htm).

Taylor, Michael Ray. *Caves: Exploring Hidden Realms.* Washington, DC: National Geographic Society, 2001.

United Nations Environment Programme. "Tassili N'Ajjer National Park, Algeria." Retrieved October 27, 2008 (http://www.unep-wcmc.org/sites/wh/tassili.html).

USGS. "Types of Caves." Retrieved October 22, 2008 (http://wrgis.wr.usgs.gov/parks/cave/#types).

World Book Online. "Carlsbad Caverns National Park." Retrieved October 26, 2008 (http://www.worldbook.com/wb/Article?id=ar095740&st=carlsbad+cavern).

World Book Online. "Cave Dwellers." Retrieved October 26, 2008 (http://www.worldbook.com/wb/Article?id=ar101180&st=prehistoric+man).

World Book Online. "Mammoth Cave National Park." Retrieved October 26, 2008 (http://www.worldbook.com/wb/Article?id=ar340980&st=mammoth+cave).

INDEX

About the Author

As a kid, Elizabeth Mills visited some show caves in her native Pennsylvania. And while researching this book, she gained a deep respect for cavers and the dangers they face in wild caves. Mills lives in Seattle, Washington, and writes all kinds of books for all kinds of kids.

Photo Credits

Cover © www.istockphoto.com/David Hogan; pp. 4–5 © David Muench/Corbis; p. 10 © Craig Lovell/Corbis; pp. 12–13, 21, 23 Wikipedia Commons; pp. 14–15 © www.istockphoto.com/Asbjorn Aakjeer; p. 16 Jerry Dodrill/Aurora/Getty Images; p. 18 NPS Photo by Peter Jones; pp. 24–25 © 2003 Kenneth Ingham; p. 27 © Francois Savigny/Minden Pictures; p. 29 © David M. Dennis/Animals Animals—Earth Scenes; p. 30 http://flickr.com/photos/timparkinson/284291008/; p. 32 © Doug Wechsler/Animals Animals—Earth Scenes; p. 34 © Pierre Andrieu/Reuters/Newscom.com; p. 36 © Kazuyoshi Nomachi/Corbis; p. 37 © www.istockphoto.com/Jarno Gonzales; p. 41 © Corbis; p. 44 Henrik Sorensen/Photonica/Getty Images; p. 46–47 Stephen Frink/Science Faction/Getty Images; p. 50 © George Steinmetz/Corbis.

Designer Les Kanturek; Editor: Bethany Bryan
Photo Researcher: Amy Feinberg